# *WEDDING* ETIQUETTE

## LINDA SONNTAG

MIMOSA
·BOOKS·

NEW YORK · AVENEL, NEW JERSEY

This 1993 edition published by Mimosa Books, distributed
by Outlet Book Company, Inc., a Random House company,
40 Engelhard Avenue, Avenel, New Jersey 07001

First published in 1991 by Grisewood & Dempsey Ltd.
Copyright © Grisewood & Dempsey Ltd. 1991

10 9 8 7 6 5 4 3 2 1

ISBN 1 85698 513 **X**

Printed and bound in Italy

# CONTENTS

# INTRODUCTION:
# WHY MARRY?

Times are changed with him who marries; there are
no more by-path meadows, where you may innocently
linger, but the road lies long and straight and dusty to
the grave.

*Robert Louis Stevenson (1850–94)*

Is marriage a field of battle or a bed of roses? Probably
it will prove to be neither. And once the bride and groom
have made their vows, will they live happily ever after,
or is that the end of their stories in another sense, and
will they spend the rest of their lives trudging the long,
straight, dusty road to the grave? Again, neither is
likely.

As recently as the 1950s, marriage was still considered
to be fundamentally a union of economic and practical
good sense. The man was the breadwinner, and the
woman kept house and brought up the children. In most
households there was a strict demarcation of tasks, and
the man did nothing in the home, unless it was heavy
work the woman couldn't manage. He knew nothing
about her domain and was hopeless at such things as for
example cooking, and sewing.

Of course, in those far distant days, marriages were
still made for love. The most common reason, now as
then, for people to marry is that they cannot bear to be
apart. But today, when women can earn as much as men
and are reaching equality in every sphere of life, the
roles of the sexes are not so clearly defined, the
dependence between them is not so great, and the
pressure on people to marry for survival, security, and
social standing has diminished.

There is another reason why marriage might be outdated. It is an institution that goes back to the beginning of recorded history when life expectancy was very short: perhaps only 25 or 30 years. Today, we in the West can expect to live to around 75. Why should a man and woman in their twenties swear to be faithful to each other for half a century or more until parted by death? Why is it that marriage is not declining in popularity?

When loves strikes, everything seems possible. Any severance of contact with the beloved seems excruciating, and the thought of a lifetime together hardly long enough. A lover wants all the world to know how he feels, and the depth of his feeling prompts him to express it in dramatic terms: "till death us do part." The truth is that most people are still idealists, especially when they are in love.

The wedding day with its pledge and symbolic ring, the fairytale dress, and all the public ceremonial that accompanies it, expresses a faith in the permanence of human feelings and a desire for perfection which are an intrinsic part of the make-up of the human being.

However, the strain of organizing a big wedding can put unnecessary pressure on the bride and groom before they have even taken their vows.

It is hoped that this book will smooth the path up the aisle toward a day that both families will look back on with pleasure, and which will be, as some do prove, the beginning of a dream come true.

# 1 GETTING ENGAGED

The idea of an engagement stems from the 6th century, when King Ethelbert of England made it illegal for a man simply to gallop up on his horse and remove the woman of his choice from her home by force. King Ethelbert was not thinking of the feelings of the woman, however, but of the loss to her father of a useful pair of hands. Any man who "stole" a woman was obliged to pay her rightful "owner" a fine of 50 shillings to compensate for all the spinning she would not now do; the unclaimed daughters of the house remained "spinsters."

This "bride price," or "wed" as it was called, sealed an agreement between the groom and the father of the bride, or sometimes between the fathers of both parties, that a marriage would take place. It is the ancestor of our engagement.

Today an engagement is not a legal requirement, and many of the trappings that surrounded the proposal of marriage and its acceptance only a hundred years ago have disappeared. The formality of the man going on bended knee in a solarium followed by an agonizing session with his prospective father-in-law, during which the groom would be grilled about his financial prospects, is no more. Today it is likely that the couple know each other well, and that they have grown toward the idea of marriage as a natural next step in their commitment to each other. Marriage is more likely to be discussed over a long period of time, rather than proposed to the accompaniment of moonlight and music; and if there is a proposal, it could as easily come from the woman as from the man.

## Telling the world

Once the decision to marry has been made, the couple may decide on an engagement as a convenient way of letting the world know their plans. It is worth remembering that a formal wedding cannot be arranged in less than three months and probably the minimum practical length of time for an engagement should be six months.

The first people to be told should be the parents of both couples. This courtesy is especially due to the parents of the bride-to-be, as the wedding may involve them in a great deal of work and expense.

Both parties will probably already know their future in-laws, and with any luck there will be a degree of mutual liking also. If there have been reservations about the suitability of the match, this is the time for parents to drop them. The decision has been made, and for the sake of future harmony, it should be welcomed with warmth. A family dinner is in order, when the couple's parents can be introduced to one another, and it is usual for the groom's parents to foot the bill if the bride's parents will be paying for the wedding.

Children should be told as soon as possible, and other relatives and close friends who would be hurt if they heard the news secondhand should be informed by letter, over the telephone, or in person. After this has been done, the couple, or the bride's parents, may decide to announce the engagement in the newspaper along the following simple lines:

SLATER – FERRY
Miss Liza Ann Slater
and Jason Alan Ferry
will be married at 3:30pm
on June 21
at First United Church in Marigold.

Details are then given of the couple's families, education, and professional information.

Engagement parties, at which the date of the wedding may be announced, are frequently held, and the bride's friends and relatives will probably plan and host all-female showers at which small gifts are given. The all-male party, called the "Honey do" (short for "Honey, do this ... and Honey, do that"), at which the groom-to-be is presented with mops and dustcloths is popular in some places.

## The ring

Giving an engagement ring is a custom that dates from Victorian times. The ring is a token of the pledge the couple makes, and, sparkling on the finger of the bride-to-be, it announces to other would-be suitors that her affections are already engaged.

Unless the fiancé is giving his betrothed a family heirloom, it is usual nowadays for the couple to choose the ring together. The idea of springing a ring on one's intended at the same time as popping the question is just not practical. Many engaged couples would rather put their money in a joint bank or savings and loan account than pay a fortune for a jewel, so it's sensible to decide in advance how much to spend.

The custom of placing the ring on the third finger of the left hand is an ancient one. The Romans believed that this finger contained the "vein of love," which ran

11

directly to the heart. A diamond is the most usual choice of stone for an engagement ring. This is partly because it is so hardwearing, but it also stems from a belief prevalent in Italy during the Middle Ages that the diamond was the stone of reconciliation and was capable of restoring harmony after a quarrel.

In recent years, coloured stones have become increasingly popular for engagements, and another option is for the bride to choose her birthstone, or another gemstone whose symbolic meaning especially appeals to her.

## Calling it off

It always takes courage to admit to a mistake, but if the mistake is an engagement that has been publicly celebrated, it takes more courage than usual. Nevertheless, a broken engagement is much less painful than a broken marriage. Friends and relatives can be told quietly and without any fuss – no explanation is due and none should be asked for, though a trusted friend may help you over a difficult time.

Presents of any value, including the ring, should be returned, if possible without rancour and recrimination – gone are the days when a jilted partner could sue for breach of promise and claim cash compensation! Early wedding presents should also be returned.

# 2 MARRIAGE, A LEGAL CONTRACT

'Married love ... is a bridal love that burns like fire and seeks nothing else but the married partner. It says: I do not want what is yours, I want neither silver nor gold, neither this nor that; I want only you yourself; I want it all or nothing. All other love seeks something other than the one it loves; this love alone wants the beloved himself.'

*Martin Luther (1483–1546)*

'We promise according to our hopes and perform according to our fears.'

*François, Duc de la Rochefoucauld (1613–80)*

As marriage is a contract recognized under law, certain conditions must be fulfilled by those entering into it, and this involves more paperwork and organization than you might think. This chapter deals as briefly as possible with the red tape.

First, you must be over your state's age limit before you can marry, and you may need your parents' consent. You must apply to the relevant city or county clerk for a licence, which is a document that legally binds the intention of two people to marry. Check with your local

Marriage Bureau to find out the exact requirements of your state. Both bride and groom must present themselves, and they must have all the relevant documents. The license is valid for a specific period – make sure to get the timing right. The license, which is usually paid for by the groom, is not valid until you are married, at which time it will be signed by the minister or the civil official who performs the ceremony.

### Church Weddings
A church wedding usually takes place in the church of either bride or groom, and one or both of the parties should have been baptized. However, some ministers are more lenient than others. If you want to marry in a different church, there may be a residency requirement. Check to see if you have to live in its vicinity for a short period, perhaps staying with a friend, though you can usually get around this requirement.

A practice known as calling the banns dates from the 14th century when cousins, however many times removed, were forbidden to marry. An announcement was made in church on three consecutive Sunday's of the couple's intention to marry. The idea was that three weeks would be time enough for the local gossips to spread the word and uncover any skeletons in the family closet. In some countries the banns are still called, but in America today the announcement of an engagement will appear in the church bulletin, but it is not a legal requirement.

### A civil ceremony
Any couple who have been granted a marriage license are free to marry anywhere they choose – at home, on a beach or a football field, in a judge's chambers or courthouse. The choice is up to you.

"A good marriage is that in which each appoints the other to be guardian of his solitude."

*Rainer Maria Rilke (1875–1926)*

## Marrying in a hurry.

English people who wanted to elope and avoid the red tape that surrounds marriage south of the border used to flee to Gretna Green, just a few miles into Scotland. There they made a declaration in front of two witnesses over the anvil in the famous blacksmith's forge and immediately became man and wife. Since 1977 Scottish marriage laws have been tightened, but tying the knot there is still a simpler process than in England.

Even simpler, and perfectly legal, is the Las Vegas wedding. All you need is a license from the county clerk, which you then take to one of the many wedding chapels in the city, where the ceremony will be over in ten minutes.

**Note**: if you plan to marry in another country, or if one of you is a foreign national, you should check carefully with the relevant consulate to make sure that the marriage will be legal in both countries and that you have all the necessary documentation before the ceremony.

## Second marriages

There is no limit to the number of times you may marry as long as you are free to do so. But there may be problems with second and subsequent marriages if you want a church wedding. For example you may only be remarried in the Roman Catholic faith if a previous marriage has been annulled, which can be a lengthy and complicated business.

## IN SOME PLACES, YOU MAY NOT MARRY YOUR ...

mother, adoptive mother, former adoptive mother, father, adoptive or former adoptive father, daughter, adoptive or former adoptive daughter, son, adoptive or former adoptive son, father's mother, father's father, mother's mother, mother's father, son's daughter, son's son, daughter's daughter, daughter's son, sister, brother, wife's mother, husband's father, wife's daughter, husband's son, father's wife, mother's husband, son's wife, daughter's husband, father's father's wife, father's mother's husband, mother's father's wife, mother's mother's husband, wife's father's mother, husband's father's father, wife's son's daughter, husband's son's son, wife's daughter's daughter, husband's daughter's son, son's son's wife, son's daughter's husband, daughter's son's wife, daughter's daughter's husband, father's sister, father's brother, mother's sister, mother's brother, brother's daughter, brother's son, sister's daughter, or sister's son.

However, it is now usually legal for a man to marry his brother's widow or for a widower to marry his dead wife's sister, or for a woman to marry her dead husband's brother or the widower of her dead sister. A divorced person can marry the sister or brother of the ex-spouse. If you fall into one of these latter categories, you may find that your minister will still refuse to marry you. Your alternatives are to look for a more understanding minister or to marry in a civil ceremony, where no objection will be raised.

## Changing your name

There is no need for the bride to take her husband's name on marriage, and women are increasingly deciding not to do so. Some feel it is demeaning and signifies a loss of identity. It may also be impractical from a career point of view. Some women decide to use both names, keeping their own name for professional use and taking their husband's name socially and on official documents. Because it can be confusing having two separate names, combine them: Fanny Godfrey Lemon. The choice is entirely up to you, but you should make your decision public immediately to avoid false assumptions.

If you want to change your name on your driver's license or passport for your honeymoon, you should apply in plenty of time.

# 3 PLANNING YOUR WEDDING

Your wedding will probably be the most spectacular celebration of your life. It is the occasion when even non-churchgoers bow to ceremonial religious tradition, when almost all the participants buy extravagant new clothes, when no expense is spared on processions of gleaming cars, mountains of food, and cases of drink, and above all when friends and family come together in your honor, to wish you happiness.

The organization of such a big, expensive and emotional day is no small task. Whatever the type of wedding and degree of formality you choose, it will need to be planned like a grand stage performance or a military campaign. The bride and her mother, by tradition the masterminds behind the operation, should be prepared to delegate as much as possible to make sure each detail is exactly as they intend it to be; then you can enjoy the wedding day, instead of tensely hoping that things will all fall into place at the last minute.

This chapter of the book aims to cover every aspect of planning a traditional church wedding, and as weddings across the religious and secular spectrum are more alike than they are different, you can use it as a guide and a checklist for the type of wedding you have chosen.

## Who picks up the tab?

This thorny question needs to be settled right at the beginning. Throughout history and all over the world, weddings have involved one party or the other in a great deal of expense. Where labor is short, the groom has to pay the bride's family a "bride price" to compensate for her loss; in rich countries it tends to be the other way around, and the bride takes a dowry to her husband.

Until fairly recently in this country, the bride's father paid all the wedding expenses, but with the increasing equality of the sexes, this custom, a direct descendant of the dowry system, is disappearing. It is quite likely today that the combined salaries of the bride and groom will exceed that of the bride's father, and that they will want to pay for much of the wedding themselves. As the person who pays gets to make the choices, this can be an advantage for the bride and groom. It is also possible that the groom's family will want to contribute something.

The important thing is that no assumptions are made and no feelings hurt. The expenses for even a small wedding are going to be considerable, and everyone should be allowed to contribute what they wish.

What follows is a guide to the traditional division of expenses among the principals. The likelihood is that you won't stick to this rigidly, but you can use the list as a basis for discussion among the family as to who will pay for what.

## Traditional Division of Wedding Expenses

**The bride's family pays for**
Newspaper announcements
Wedding stationery (invitations, place cards etc.)
Bride's dress, veil, and accessories
Groom's gift and ring
Organist and soloist
Wedding day transportation (except going-away car and groom's car)
Reception: rental of sites, food, wine, cake, entertainment

Photographs and video
Gifts for all women attendants
Accommodation for out-of-town bridal attendants

**The bridegroom pays for**
Bride's engagement and wedding rings
Clergy fees
Marriage license
All flowers
Presents for best man, ushers
His own car to the church
The going-away car
Accommodation for out-of-town ushers
The honeymoon

**The bride pays for**
The groom's ring, if he wants one

**The groom's attendants pay for**
Their own clothes
Traveling expenses
A wedding gift

**The bride's attendants pay for**
Their own clothes (parents pay for children)
Traveling expenses
A wedding gift

## Choosing your attendants
The idea of having attendants at a wedding – maid of honor and bridesmaids, best man and ushers – originated with the belief that evil spirits, envious of the couple's happiness, would be out to harm them, but would be confused by the presence of so many similarly dressed people.

Though evil spirits are no longer feared, the quality of selflessness is still most valued in wedding attendants. The bride will probably want to choose her closest friend as **maid of honor**; she will help with arrangements, offer moral support, help dress the bride, hold the bouquet while the bride signs the certificate and help look after the other attendants and the older guests at the reception, as well as enjoying herself. A married friend is called a **matron of honor**.

A bride can have any number of **bridesmaids**, though most have fewer than five, and usually at least one small child is chosen to be a **flower girl or page**.

The **ushers** are close male friends of the groom, chosen for their friendliness and unflappability. Their role is to usher people to their seats in the church, and hand out the hymnbooks. They should be armed with umbrellas to escort people to and from the wedding cars in case it rains, (some say a sign of luck). At the reception they should be ready to talk to guests who look stranded, make introductions, and offer food and drink.

The **best man** is a key figure at any wedding. The bride's mother is planner-in-chief, but on the wedding day itself the best man takes over as prime organizer behind the scenes. His first duty is to be the "guardian" to the groom, to see that he gets to the right place at the right time, to hand the ring or rings to the minister on cue, to take charge of the groom's transportation and help the guests with parking, and to deliver a good speech at the reception. In addition, he may organize a bachelor party beforehand, and play master of ceremonies and introduce speakers at the reception.

All this requires a cool head, and if the groom's best friend is absent-minded, easily distracted, or likely to succumb to too much champagne before his duties are over, then it might be wiser to give the job to someone more reliable and let the best friend concentrate on enjoying himself.

See pages 90-93 for the individual duties of each participant before and on the day.

## Dressing up for the wedding

> Married in white, you have chosen alright
> Married in green, ashamed to be seen
> Married in gray, you will go far away
> Married in red, you will wish yourself dead
> Married in blue, love ever true
> Married in yellow, you're ashamed of your fellow
> Married in black, you'll wish yourself back
> Married in pink, your spirits will sink
> Married in brown, you'll live out of town
> Married in pearl, you'll live in a whirl.

One of the first things you will want to do when you have decided the date of your wedding is to organize your outfit, whether it's rented, bought, or made. Allow as much time as possible to make the right choice, and remember that you may need several fittings. Wedding stores stock only sample outfits, and dresses must be special ordered.

White wedding dresses have been in the forefront of bridal fashion since Queen Victoria of England broke with the royal tradition of a silver dress and opted for white for her wedding to Prince Albert in 1840. The links between the snowy purity of the wedding dress and the virginity of its wearer have largely been forgotten, and there is no reason why you should not choose a traditional white dress even if you are pregnant, or if the maid of honor is your daughter. Equally, a virginal bride may choose to wear another colour; oyster has been a particular favorite since the wedding of Britain's Princess Diana in 1981.

If the fairytale look is not for you, then you may choose an elegant outfit of any color, perhaps a suit or a stunning dress and jacket. This would also make a good choice for a going-away outfit. If the wedding is not in a church, simplicity may be your keynote. The important thing is that you look and feel your best.

Of course it is not necessary to wear anything at all on your head, but most brides choose some ornament, whether it is a full veil, dashing hat, or just a single flower. Obviously your choice of **headgear** should complement your dress and to some extent dictate your hairstyle, but you should beware of torturing your hair into an elaborate and unnatural style on this of all days.

If you do want to wear your **hair** differently – say in a topknot secured with flowers – try it out several times beforehand to make sure you like it, and be guided by the groom's reaction: if he thinks it looks a mess, you'd probably better forget it. Think, too, about what you'll do with your hair after the reception, when you change into your going-away clothes. If the style you've chosen looks fine with a tiara and veil, but collapses without them, you may want to reconsider. Generally speaking, if you choose your headgear to suit your normal hairstyle and not the other way around, you won't go far wrong.

**Make-up** is another area potentially full of pitfalls for the bride. Again, the less of it you can get away with, the better. This is not the occasion to try out false eyelashes for the first time (they are bound to fall off, or at the very least make your eyes water) or to go wild with bright red lipstick – there will be lots of people kissing you, and it will smudge. Remember that you will be in the public eye for a good number of hours, and that you will probably get quite hot with excitement. Put on your make-up with a light hand, and avoid greasy make-up that will "crease."

### Dressing the other key figures

The **bridal attendants** – maid of honor, bridesmaids, flower girl, and ring bearer usually wear clothes which they or their parents pay for, so, unless their outfits are rented, it is sensible to choose dresses and suits that can be worn again and are not too expensive. The chief requirement is that they look good grouped around the bride.

The **groom** and **best man**, as well as the other chief male guests, normally wear a tuxedo at a formal wedding, though for a more modest church or civil ceremony, dark suits are appropriate.

The **mothers of the bride and groom** will want to look their best, though they must be careful not to try to upstage the bride: plunging necklines and feather boas should be kept for another occasion. It is useful for the two mothers to compare notes so that their outfits are neither identical nor absurdly different in style or degree of formality.

## The flowers

### If Love

If love were what the rose is,
And I were like the leaf,
Our lives would grow together
In sad or singing weather,
Blown fields or flowerful closes,
Green pleasure or gray grief;
If love were what the rose is,
And I were like the leaf.

*Algernon Charles Swinburne (1837–1909)*

Flowers have always played a central role in weddings. At Anglo-Saxon marriage ceremonies, both bride and groom wore garlands, and in the Middle Ages it was common for the garlands to be entwined with ears of wheat symbolizing fertility. This century, until recently, it was thought obligatory for brides to carry white bouquets and wear garlands of orange blossom (the flower of virginity), but now almost anything goes, even garden flowers or wild flowers (though be warned that many wild flowers wilt very quickly).

Ideally, all the flowers should be ordered from the same florist so that there is continuity from the boutonnieres right through to the church flowers and the arrangements (if any) at the reception.

Your choice of flowers may be elaborate, or simple. They should reflect the mood of the occasion, the style of your dress, and most important of all, your own personality. There is a special pleasure in using seasonal flowers, which often costs less too.

Always consult the minister before planning the church decorations. Yours may not be the only wedding on the chosen day, and you may be able to share the cost of church flowers with the other bridegrooms. You will also need to find out if there are regular volunteer flower arrangers. If so, they may decorate the church for you, and you can offer a donation to show your gratitude. But they may not be up to the professional standard of the florist, and if you want swags and pew-end nosegays, this could be a consideration.

**The bride's flowers** are going to be the center of attention and need to be chosen with great care. They may dictate the theme for all the other flowers for the day. You will want to feel comfortable holding them (it will give you something to do with your hands!), and of course they must complement your dress. If possible, take a sample of the fabric and a sketch of the dress to your florist. If it's a long dress with a sweeping train, you will need a fairly large bouquet to balance the effect; a short dress will look better with a smaller nosegay. A single flower attached to a prayer book is beautifully simple and less expensive.

**Bridal flowers**

1. Single bloom with prayer book
2. Circular nosegay
3. Nosegay with trailing ribbons
4. Simple spray
5. Teardrop or fall
6. Trailing teardrop

## The photographs

Your wedding photographs should be something that you can always look back on with pleasure, so it really is important to choose a professional to take them, unless you know someone who is especially talented with a camera. Your friends' snapshots may be amusing, but the laughter would probably not be quite so high-spirited if the only image you had of yourselves on this supreme occasion was a headless blurr.

The photographer needs to be booked well in advance, particularly if you are getting married on a Saturday. Prices can vary so shop around. Personal recommendations count for a lot, and samples of the photographer's work should be available for inspection. Some photographers offer package deals, with a flat fee for the day and a separate charge for the number of prints ordered; others itemize each operation; others still may offer "special effects": misty finishes, photographs printed on champagne glasses, etc.

Any professional photographer will know how to set up group portrait photographs of the principal participants. Beyond that, you will need to decide whether to include candid shots of the bride at home before the ceremony, and whether you want photographs of the reception and departure for the honeymoon. You could also consider informal shots: Uncle Wilfred dozing off while the best man drones on; Aunt Wilhelmina losing her hat to a gust of wind, etc. These shots sometimes best capture the spirit of the day.

Check with the minister whether photographs are permitted inside the church. Some may forbid photography during the ceremony itself. Guests with cameras should also make sure that photography in the church is welcome before they begin to snap away. Some brides, as well as ministers, resent the intrusion of a flashbulb while they are saying their vows. Don't let the photographs take too much time. Discuss with the photographer exactly where they are to be taken, and who will be in each group. Too many posed photographs outside the church can lead to awkward lines of people waiting to leave, and if they are taken before guests are greeted at the reception, there may again be a boring wait.

## Videos

Videos are increasingly popular wedding souvenirs. Visit several firms and see examples of their work before you make a decision. Pay particular attention to the quality of sound, the continuity, and the naturalness or otherwise of members of the wedding party: no one wants a cameraman who makes your friends feel self-conscious.

Some firms offer a make-up service for the bride in with the price. Consider whether you want this: you may feel less like an actress and more like yourself if you put on your own make-up as usual.

Consult the minister to see if the service can be filmed. If so, arrange to visit the church with the technician to finalize the position of lights, microphones, and wires: they should be as unobtrusive as possible. Perhaps the videographer can attend the rehearsal to determine where to put the cameras and people.

## Music

Bells were once rung at weddings to ward off the evil spirits, but now people usually pay for the organist by making a contribution to the church.

The music in a typical church ceremony should build up to a resounding climax. The organ plays as people are finding their seats. The music needs to be robust enough to drown out settling-down noises, and it should be positive, expectant, and joyous in tone. The next stage is the entrance of the bride: the moment everyone has been waiting for. The bride should practice walking to her chosen wedding march piece to make sure the pace is right, and that it is neither too long nor too short to get her up the aisle.

If you have a soloist, you must choose the music together and make sure that you are both happy with the order in which things will happen. Make sure, too, that the soloist and organist have time to rehearse together.

Finally, comes the rousing recessional, the triumphant progress of bride and groom back down the aisle.

When to her lute Corinna sings,
Her voice revives the leaden strings,
And both in highest notes appear
As any challenged echo clear.
But when she doth of mourning speak,
E'en with her sighs the strings do break.

And as her lute doth live or die,
Led by her passion, so must I.
For when of pleasure she doth sing,
My thoughts enjoy a sudden spring;
But if she doth of sorrow speak,
E'en from my heart the strings do break.

*Thomas Campion (1567–1620)*

31

# WEDDING MUSIC

When making your selection, bear in mind the capabilities of organist and soloist as well as the size and acoustics of the church. Old favorites will probably be more appreciated than unfamiliar pieces.

## Before the service
Bach: Jesu, Joy of Man's Desiring
Elgar: "Nimrod" from the Enigma Variations
Handel: Water Music
Purcell: Prelude in G
Bach: Sheep May Safely Graze
Brahms: Behold A Rose Is Blooming
    How Lovely Is Thy Dwelling Place
Handel: "Minuet" from *Berenice*
Albinoni: Adagio in G Minor
Mozart: Romanze from *Eine Kleine Nachtmusik*
Schubert: Ave Maria
Vaughan-Williams: Chorale Prelude on Rhosmedre

## The entrance of the bride
Bliss: A Wedding Fanfare
Beethoven: "Hallelujah Chorus" from *The Mount of Olives*
Brahms: Theme from the St. Anthony Chorale
Charpentier: Prelude to a Te Deum
Guilmant: Lift Up Your Heads
Handel: Arrival of the Queen of Sheba
Stanley: Trumpet Voluntary from the Suite in D
Wagner: "Bridal March" from *Lohengrin*
Harris: Wedding Processional

## The procession down the aisle
Dubois: Toccata in D
Elgar: Pomp and Circumstance No. 4
Harris: Flourish For An Occasion
Parry: Bridal March
Purcell: Trumpet Tune
Whitlock: Fanfare
Mendelssohn: Wedding March from *A Midsummer Night's Dream*
Walton: Crown Imperial
Boyce: Trumpet Voluntary
Widor: Toccata

## The Music of Love

How oft, when thou, my music, music play'st
Upon that blessed wood whose motion sounds
With thy sweet fingers, when thou gently sway'st
The wiry concord that mine ear confounds,
Do I envy those jacks that nimble leap
To kiss the tender inward of thy hand,
Whilst my poor lips, which should that harvest reap,
At the wood's boldness by thee blushing stand.
To be so tickled, they would change their state
And situation with those dancing chips
O'er whom thy fingers walk with gentle gait,
Making dead wood more blest than living lips.
Since saucy jacks so happy are in this,
Give them thy fingers, me thy lips to kiss.

*William Shakespeare (1564–1616)*

## Transportation

If you want to rent a traditional limosine, look in the
Yellow Pages to find a list of firms. Some brides like the
novelty of a vintage car or a horse-drawn carriage, which
are likely to be even more expensive than a Rolls-Royce
or Bentley. The alternative is to use the cars of family
or friends, giving them a good polish and decorating
them if you wish. A token thank-you present to the
owners, who will probably be delighted to be asked in
the first place, will be cheaper than paying a hire firm.

You will need two or three bridal cars: one for the
bride and her father, one for the bridal attendants and
possibly one for the bride's mother and a companion.
The best man usually drives the groom to the church in
his own car.

After the ceremony, the bride and groom are driven

to the reception in the first car, followed by the bridal attendants. Make sure the bride's parents have transportation. The bride and groom will also need transportation to their honeymoon destination, or to a rail station or airport. No one who has been drinking should be allowed to drive. It is a good idea to hide the getaway car unless you enjoy the idea of having it turned into an advertisement of your newly married state.

### Daisy

Daisy, Daisy,
Give me your answer, do!
I'm half crazy,
All for the love of you.
It won't be a stylish marriage
I can't afford a carriage
But you'll look sweet
Upon the seat
Of a bicycle made for two.

## The invitations

Ideally, your guests should receive their invitations about six weeks before the wedding, allow eight weeks if the wedding day is during a holiday period. But a lot has to happen before the invitation arrives. Traditionally the bride's mother works out the guest list, first determining how many people the budget can cater for (see page 39). The groom and his mother give their list of guests to her. Order more invitations than you think you'll need. The attendant and their parents, everyone in the groom's family, and the minister and spouse should be sent an invitation, and you will want a few as keepsakes. Order extra envelopes to allow for the inevitable spoilage.

Engraved or printed invitations should be ordered in advance. The stationer will show you a selection of samples, but generally the wording is as follows:

> *Mr. and Mrs. Alfred Sidelock*
> *request the pleasure of your company*
> *at the marriage of their daughter*
> *Elsie*
> *to*
> *Lt. Joseph Brown*
> *at the First Ecumenical Congregation,*
> *Upper Glenfield*
> *on Saturday November 9 1995*
> *at three o'clock*
> *and after at*
> *The Manor, Glenfield*
>
> *R.S.V.P.*
> *103 Stateline Road*
> *Tweedale*

The name of the guest is handwritten in the top left-hand corner.

Naturally, if one or both parents of the bride are not hosting the reception, other names will appear at the head of the invitation, but if one or both parents act as hosts, even if they are not paying for the festivities, the invitations should still come from them. In the case of divorced parents, both names should appear, if both will be there to welcome the guests. If the bride and groom are giving the reception themselves, in the case of a second marriage perhaps, their names will appear. It is really a matter of combining tact with common sense.

Make sure the addresses of the sites of the ceremony and the reception are given in full, and if there could be any difficulty in finding them, enclose a map.

If it is a civil wedding, most of the invitations will be to the reception only. If it is a big wedding with a lunchtime reception and a party in the evening, you may want to invite two entirely different sets of guests.

### Wedding presents

Every guest invited to the wedding normally gives a present. Some of your close friends and family will have very definite ideas about what they want to give you, but the majority will just want to please, and the best way to help them, and avoid ending up with a houseful of irons and no toaster, is to make a present list.

If you send out a present list to each person who requests one, you may still end up with duplicate presents. The list should be registered with one or more local stores, and you should specify the make and pattern of items that you would like. Guests can choose a present at the store, and the present can be checked off the list. Or, even easier, they can consult the list, order by telephone, and pay by credit card.

Make sure your list includes a variety of prices, so that everyone can find a suitable and affordable gift.

If you already have a home and don't need an iron or a toaster, you might suggest plants for the garden, books, wine, or C.D.s. It used to be considered bad taste for anyone other than close family to give money, but if it is offered, why not waive the rules and enjoy it?

Remember to make a note of each present and who gave it as soon as it arrives, so that you can write a thank-you letter when you get the chance. Better to write them before the wedding than after, if you get the time; if you're settling into a new home on your return from honeymoon, there probably won't be much to spare time.

Presents are usually put on display for the guests to see, particularly if the reception is at the bride's mother's home. Remember that this practice can cause embarrassment and hurt feelings.

It is customary for the key people in the wedding party to exchange **lasting mementos**. Bride and groom exchange gifts, the groom's parents give something to the bride, the bride's parents give something to the groom. The groom gives presents to his best man, and the ushers, and the bride gives gifts to her attendants.

In this welter of gift-giving it might be easy to overlook the person who may have worked the hardest and deserve the most appreciation, the bride's mother. The bride, the groom, and her husband should all try to show their gratitude, remembering that at the end of the day, even though it has been a great success, she will probably be feeling drained and more than a little sad.

# 4 PLANNING THE RECEPTION

A large formal wedding will usually be followed by a lavish reception, but there is no reason why a small simple wedding should not also lead to a grand party: it is a matter of taste, and, of course, of expense. At one end of the scale is the full wedding meal, which could take place in a hotel, on a river boat or under a canopy in the backyard; then there is the buffet lunch, which could be held in a club or hall; and, cheapest and most intimate, canapés and champagne at home. There is no need to have a formal meal; a selection of canapés, perhaps with strawberries and cream to follow, is quite usual at even the most fashionable weddings. The time of the wedding ceremony will influence your choice; a formal meal may be inappropriate in mid-afternoon! The entertainment may also be in two stages, with a lunchtime spread for the family followed by an evening party with music and dancing for friends.

If money is no object, there are firms that will take care of every detail, the reception, including cake, flowers, music, and champagne; they will also book your reception whether it be in a hotel, a museum or a beautiful house.

In the medium price range, the most important decision you will have to make is whether to do the cooking yourselves or engage someone to do it for you. It goes without saying that cooking for even 30 people is a mammoth task that few would relish, particularly on top of all the other responsibilities of the wedding day. To employ a good caterer, even for a buffet at home, could be money well spent.

## The seating plan

Wherever the reception is held, certain seating requirements may need to be fulfilled. Traditionally, tables are arranged so that as many people as possible can see the bride, groom, and speakers without craning their necks. If you are having a stand-up buffet, seats should be provided for old or infirm relatives; and you may also need to set aside an area with high chairs, for young children, and maybe a room where babies can be breast-fed and changed.

For a formal reception, the bridal party usually sits along one side only of the top table, where they can see and be seen. The table may be on a stage or dais if the room has one. The bride and groom sit in the center, preferably not obscured behind a towering cake, with the other key figures to their left and right.

Best man

Groom's mother

Bride's father

Bride

Groom

Bride's mother

Groom's father

Maid of honor

If one or both sets of parents have divorced and remarried, then provided that there is room, all the parents and step-parents should take their places on the top table. This may require some careful thinking to work out a tactful seating arrangement. Place step-parents together, and partners of first marriages apart. If a parent has been divorced or bereaved and has no new partner, then a suitable companion should be found to lighten the occasion for him or her.

The trouble with having a "top table," apart from the possible friction between divorced parties and irritation on the part of those who feel they should be sitting at it but aren't, is that it is cut off from the rest of the party. As conversation can be only with the person on your right or on your left, and not even with both at the same time, half the table may be eating in silence at any one moment, and it is quite possible that the rest of the guests will be having far more fun than those stuck up at the front in a line staring down at them. The solution can be to have a roomful of round tables, and this, combined with short speeches which mean only minimal neck-craning and interruption of conversation, can make for a much more successful party than the traditional arrangement.

As for the seating at the other tables, this should not prove problematical, as long as you put guests in groups of friends, and older relations who have not seen each other for a long time, and make a good mix of men and women, so that everyone has a maximum opportunity for enjoying the occasion. Remember that a wedding is not always a happy event for single people, who may feel that all the world is married but themselves. If possible, try to seat them next to other single people they might like.

It is a good idea to pin a copy of the seating plan on

a board inside the room where everyone can see it, but not at the doorway, where it will cause a bottleneck and hold up the receiving line (see page 73).

### The site

If you decide on a **hotel**, visit two or three likely ones and check out the following points:

* Does the price include rental of the room, as well as food?
* Is the food of the right standard and price?
* Does the hotel provide flowers?
* Will an M.C. be available?
* What about a cake?
* Do you like the atmosphere of the room?
* Are the cloakroom facilities adequate?
* Will there be somewhere for the bride to change?
* Is this a good place to spend your honeymoon, or at least the first night, or will you be traveling on?

If you choose a room in a **local club**, ask yourself:

* Will it be warm enough?
* Will it be gloomy?
* Will it be comfortable?
* Is there adequate parking?
* What are the restrooms like?
* Are there adequate kitchen facilities for the caterers?
* Will china, glasses, and silverware be provided?
* If you are planning on having music, how will this be arranged?
* Will you need to take out insurance?
* At what time must you vacate the building?
* Who will clean up?

If you are entertaining **at home**, ask yourself:

* Is there room?
* Will the caterer provide china, glasses, and silverware?
* Will you need to protect your furniture, carpets, etc., from spills?
* How will you accommodate any children?
* Where will the guests park?
* Will the caterers wash the dishes?

## Food to serve at a wedding

The food should be both delicious and practical. If you choose chicken salad, make sure your caterer's standard recipe is a good one. Appetizers should be designed so that they do not fall to pieces en route to the guest's mouth. Inevitably, some guests will have traveled a long way to see you, so make sure if you're providing finger food that there's also something a little more substantial, such as a good selection of bread and cheese.

Remember to consider everyone's tastes. You may adore curry, but Uncle Wilfred and Aunt Wilhelmina may not. Don't forget that some of your guests may be vegetarian or vegan, and others may be prevented from eating certain foods because of an allergy or religious beliefs.

The **cake** will be the focal point of your reception. The tradition of wedding cake dates back at least to the Romans, who ate a "cake" made of flour, salt, and water while the marriage ceremony was being performed. Small cakes were once thrown like confetti over the bride, or by the bride's attendants to the other witnesses of her marriage. The idea of a tiered and frosted confection came from France after 1660; originally the cake was broken open over the bride's head, whereupon lots of tiny cakes would fall out. Luckily today we have developed pleasanter ways of wishing the bride well.

Whether you choose a many-tiered frosted cake or a simpler one, the tradition is for the bride and groom to cut it together, with his hand over hers, and feed each other a slice, as a symbol of the sharing of worldly goods. It might be a good idea to make the cut beforehand and disguise it under some decoration. After the first cut has been made, the cake is usually taken behind the scenes to be cut up into slices, which are then handed out to the guests. You may like to send absent friends a small piece of cake in a little box. (If so, remember to order the cake boxes along with all the other stationery.) Single people are by tradition supposed to put a slice of wedding cake under their pillow, because it will in theory make them dream about the person they will marry.

Wedding cakes are very expensive, and one way to save on the cost of your reception is to make your own, or to ask a friend or relative to do it for you as their contribution to the day's festivities. A homemade cake can be much nicer than a bought one, especially if it carries the good wishes of someone close to you.

The wedding cake can be served as dessert at the reception, and often the top layer is removed and frozen to be eaten on the couple's first anniversary.

### Cutting the cake

Wedding cake is traditionally served in square pieces, or small slices. The information in this table will help you calculate what size cake you need, based on the number of guests you have invited. Don't forget to allow for extra pieces to send to absent friends and relatives.

| Size of cake | No. of slices |
| --- | --- |
| 5 inch round | 7 |
| 5 inch square | 8 |
| 6 inch round | 11 |
| 6 inch square | 14 |
| 7 inch round | 15 |
| 7 inch square | 20 |
| 8 inch round | 20 |
| 8 inch square | 27 |
| 9 inch round | 27 |

| Size of cake | No. of slices |
|---|---|
| 9 inch square | 35 |
| 10 inch round | 34 |
| 10 inch square | 45 |
| 11 inch round | 43 |
| 11 inch square | 56 |
| 12 inch round | 50 |
| 12 inch square | 67 |

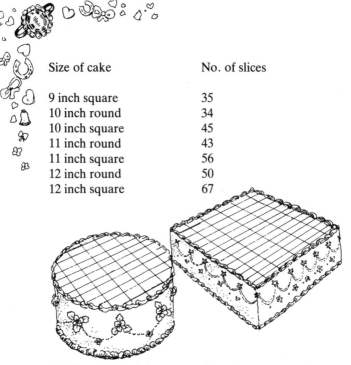

▲ *There is much less waste if a cake is cut in slices as illustrated, rather than in wedges, and as you can see, a square cake is better value than a round one.*

**Drink to serve at a wedding**

Champagne is the best possible drink for a wedding. To make it go farther, you could begin by serving mimosa – equal quantities of chilled champagne and orange juice – then go on to white wine, saving the "neat" champagne for the toasts. sparkling wines make a good substitute at less than half the price, but be sure to sample several first: they can be unpleasantly sweet. You can also serve sparkling cider or punch for the toast.

Offer dry and medium dry wines. White wine is usually drunk at twice the rate of red. A safe choice of liquor is whiskey, but make sure there are plenty of soft drinks and mineral water for drivers, teetotallers, and children. Coffee and tea – perhaps also a herbal tea – should be offered at the end of the meal.

If you are ordering in bulk from a liqour store, you can probably arrange to return any liquor that has not been opened. As a rough idea, allow about half a bottle of wine per person, slightly more if the guests are sitting down. If the caterers are serving at a stand-up buffet, agree in advance on how quickly you want them to refill glasses.

# 5 COUNTDOWN TO THE DAY

This section of the book is designed to help you plan your wedding with the minimum of fuss. Whatever type of wedding you choose, it could turn into an organizational nightmare unless each part of your plan dovetails with the next. The bigger the wedding, the worse the mess you could find yourselves in. So check off the boxes as you complete each task, or strike them off if they don't apply, and you will be able to see at a glance what remains to be done.

The first priority is for the bride and groom to name the date. Bear in mind that the peak wedding season is from July to September, though June and December are also busy months. You will need to make your plans well in advance. Three months is the absolute minimum of time in which a big wedding can be successfully arranged, though you might get away with less in the winter.

## As early as possible
☐ Draw up a budget, deciding on the size and type of wedding, and the number of guests.

☐ Set the date, reserve the church and minister, or judge, and the site for the reception.

☐ Choose your attendants – best man, maid of honor, etc. – and get their acceptance.

☐ Draw up the guest list.

☐ Reserve your wedding day limosines.

☐ Reserve the photographer and video company (if you want one).

☐ Make reservations for your honeymoon. Order a passport, if necessary, and arrange to have your name changed on your passport if you want.

48

☐ Order your cake.

☐ Decide on and buy or arrange to rent the wedding dress and headdress, or place the order with a dressmaker.

☐ Decide on and arrange the attendants' outfits, or place an order with the dressmaker.

☐ Buy or arrange to rent the groom's clothes, or check over those he means to wear.

☐ Visit the minister and discuss the arrangements.

☐ Reserve the organist and soloist.

☐ Choose the wedding music.

☐ Arrange the entertainment for the reception, if required. Discuss the order of the service and the wording of prayers, etc.

☐ Reserve the caterer for the reception, if required.

☐ Hire musicians or D.J.

☐ Order the wedding invitations (they may take several weeks).

☐ Order the stationery, such as cake boxes, seating cards, at home cards, and formals and informals.

☐ Reserve the florist.

## Well in advance

☐ Draw up your wedding present list and place it with suitable stores.

☐ Buy the wedding ring or rings.

☐ Decide on the food and drink for the reception.

☐ Decide on your trousseau, including your honeymoon clothes, and your wedding accessories, such as shoes and underwear.

☐ Arrange the rehearsal in the church, synagogue, or mosque.

☐ Plan pre-wedding parties including the rehearsal supper.

☐ Reserve a hotel room for the wedding night.

☐ Speak to both mothers about their outfits, to make sure that they are compatible.

☐ Send out your invitations at least six weeks ahead.

☐ Choose gifts for the key members of the wedding party.

☐ If you need to be immunized before your honeymoon, get this done early, as it may make you feel terrible afterwards.

☐ If you need it, get family planning advice.

**Six weeks before**

☐ Apply for your marriage license. Regulations vary from state to state.

☐ Check that all your invitations have been answered: if any are outstanding, check that they have been received.

☐ Confirm arrangements with photographer, florist, limo company, dress and caterers.

☐ Check that the wedding dress and headgear are perfect in all their details.

☐ Wear your wedding shoes around the house to get used to them. Shoes that don't feel comfortable would be excruciating on the day.

☐ Practice walking in your dress and veil or train.

☐ Practice getting in and out of a car, in a simulated veil and train. (You won't want to risk your veil and dress getting torn or dirty, so use a piece of net and a sheet pinned to length. If you don't want anyone to see you and your garage is too small to maneuver in, get someone to hold a tray over your head to represent the roof of the car while you're sitting down, and practice indoors.)

☐ Try out hairstyles, and reserve a stylist if necessary.

☐ Make a seating plan for the reception if necessary.

☐ Give final numbers to caterers as soon as possible.

☐ Double-check your honeymoon arrangements.

☐ Make arrangements for guests to stay overnight if they are traveling some distance.

☐ Make a record of the gifts you receive and write thank-you letters as presents arrive.

☐ The bride should arrange for her change of name to take place after the wedding day on official documents (bank account, driver's license, etc.), if she wants.

## The week before

☐ Arrange your blood tests if required by your state.

☐ Confirm any outstanding arrangements as early as possible.

☐ Try on the wedding dress in case you have lost or gained weight. Child bridesmaids' dresses should also be checked in case they have grown.

☐ Arrange times to take delivery of the wedding dress and bouquet, the groom's and bridesmaids' outfits, boutonnieres, corsages, to be delivered etc.

☐ Attend the rehearsal.

☐ Make sure everyone knows what their duties will be on the day, and that the groom and best man have prepared speeches.

☐ Make sure the cake has been delivered.

☐ Make sure the best man has organized your going-away car.

☐ Confirm the exact time with the limosine company, once you have timed the journey yourself in similar traffic conditions.

## The day before

☐ Pack for the honeymoon.

☐ Make sure the bride's mother or the maid of honor has an emergency kit (tissues, needle and thread, make-up) on hand.

☐ Make sure the dress is ready to put on, and not creased.

☐ Transfer the bride's engagement ring to the right hand.

☐ Make sure the best man has the ring(s) in a safe place.

# 6 PRE-NUPTIAL PARTIES AND THE REHEARSAL

The run-up to your wedding will no doubt involve a round of parties and entertaining by friends and relatives who want to wish you well in your new life together.

## Showers

Most brides will be given one or more showers. They can be lunches, suppers, afternoon teas, or coffee mornings and may be informal buffets or seated formal meals, but are just as likely to be simple get-togethers with refreshments. After all, the purpose of a shower is to supply the couple with useful items for their new life together.

Shower hostesses usually choose a theme, with decorations and food planned around it, and presents chosen to fit in.

## Parties

Friends or relatives who host a party for you as a couple may choose anything from an intimate dinner to a dance. You should be careful to avoid tiring yourselves out before the big day. Perhaps some of the entertaining can be scheduled after the honeymoon, when the excitement has died down a little.

## The bridal luncheon

During the week before the wedding, there is traditionally a party for the "ladies" only, attended by the bride and her attendants, the mothers of both the bride and the groom, and the grandmothers of the couple.

This is a good moment for the bride to present her attendants with their gifts if she chooses.

## The rehearsal

The day before the wedding, there should be a full rehearsal of the entire wedding held in the place where the ceremony will take place. All members of the wedding party, including the musicians should attend.

Follow the exact order of the ceremony as strictly as possible, but try to avoid tiring out any young children who are taking part. In most cases, the occasion will be a typical "dress rehearsal" with mistakes and kerfuffles. Keep your sense of humor; it will almost always be fine on the day, and some of the fondest memories later will come from things that didn't go quite as they were planned.

## The rehearsal party

Everyone who takes part in the wedding ceremony should be invited to this celebration, which is usually hosted (and paid for) by the groom's family. It takes place after the rehearsal on the day before the wedding. Invitations do not need to be formal, but some form of invitation should be issued to all the participants. This is another good occasion for giving presents to the attedants if this has not been done before.

## The bachelor party

For many people, the purpose of bachelor parties, which are traditionally arranged by the best man, is to get the groom-to-be drunk, and for this reason it is wise never to hold them on the night before the wedding. These are the occasions when friends sometimes play tricks; the groom risks being the butt of some pretty adolescent pranks. In primitive terms, this evening represents a shaking out of the evil spirits that could yet get in the way of the couple's marriage: once it is over, it should be plain sailing to the wedding day itself.

# 7 THE WEDDING DAY

By the time the wedding day arrives, all the arrangements should have fallen perfectly into place. Provided the participants remember their roles and stick to the schedule that has been worked out for them, it should be the wonderful day that you have all worked so hard for.

There are more similarities in the wedding services of the various faiths than there are differences between them. The bride wears a traditional dress and veil; her father accompanies her up the aisle. In a Roman Catholic wedding, however, there is no giving-away. The Quaker ceremony does not specify rings, though most Quaker brides still choose to wear one; indeed, rings are becoming more common for both parties in any denomination.

For the bride, the wedding begins with dressing, traditionally done under the watchful eyes of her mother and the maid of honor. While the bride is getting dressed, her bouquet and the flowers for any other members of the party present in the house should be delivered by the florist. Phone the florist immediately if

these are late, and once they arrive, put them in a cool place (small nosegays, corsages and boutonnieres in the refrigerator) until the last minute.

Once the dress is on, and the bride is wearing "something old, something new, something borrowed, and something blue," her hair and headdress are arranged, and the finishing touches have been made to her make-up, the first photographs of the day can be taken with the mother of the bride and the maid of honor. Make sure you have arranged for the photographer to come at least half an hour before the wedding car is due.

---

### SEQUENCE FOR ARRIVAL AT THE CHURCH

* Ushers arrive and distribute service sheets 30 minutes before the ceremony.
* Organist begins playing 30 minutes beforehand.
* Groom and best man arrive 20 minutes beforehand.
* Guests arrive at least 15 minutes beforehand.
* Bride's mother arrives 5 minutes beforehand.
* Bridal attendants arrive 5 minutes beforehand and line up inside the door to wait for the bride.

---

**The entrance of the bride**

The bride drives to church with her father, or with a close male friend of the family or relative. Nowadays, the bride's mother performs this function if the bride's father, for one reason or another, is not there. When her car pulls up outside the church, an usher opens the car door and helps her out, or she waits for her father to get out and help her. All eyes are on the bride, and the everyday action of getting out of the car without either hunching herself up in an ungainly fashion, or losing her headdress, can be quite tricky, as many a wedding video proves. This is definitely something to practice beforehand, so the wedding can get off to a smooth start.

The bride's father offers her his right arm, and they progress to the door of the church. Just inside the church door, the maid of honor arranges the bride's train and checks that she has her engagement ring on her right hand. An usher, or an assistant minister gives a sign to the organist, who strikes up the processional music, whereupon the congregation rises as the bride and her father begin to move up the aisle, at the pace they have practiced, and the attendants fall in neatly behind, thus:

Bridesmaids
Maid of honor
Flower girl + Ring bearer
Bride + Bride's father

In some cases, the minister stands at the door to greet the bride and processes up the aisle in front of her, but more often he waits at the altar. In some countries, the groom waits at the door and walks up the aisle with the bride, but in traditional American ceremonies he waits at the altar facing the bride, with the best man at his right side.

When the bride reaches the groom, she hands her bouquet to the maid of honor, who holds it for her during the ceremony. (If there is no attendant, she may give it to her father, who will pass it to her mother for safekeeping.) At this moment she may lift her veil, perhaps with the help of the maid of honor, so that the groom will be able to see her face as they exchange vows.

## Traditional Christian wedding ceremony

In some denominations the bride's father sits beside his wife during the ceremony. In others he stays by the bride's side until she has been "given away." The maid of honor remains standing behind the bride, and the other attendants line up before the altar in the formation arranged and practiced at the rehearsal.

The service will then follow according to the plan explained by the minister at the rehearsal. It usually begins with a prayer, and then the minister addresses the bridegroom, and asks him:

"Do you take this woman to be your wedded wife, to live together according to God's holy law in the state of matrimony? Will you love her, comfort her, honor and keep her in sickness and in health and, forsaking all others, keep you only to her, so long as you both shall live?"

The bridegroom answers: "I do." The minister then asks similar questions of the bride, and she answers: "I do."

The minister then asks: "Who gives this woman to be married to this man?" The bride's father does not need to say anything – he merely gives the bride's right hand, palm down, to the minister, who puts it in the hand of the groom. Some couples prefer to leave out this "giving away" part of the ceremony, as it harks back to the time when a woman was considered no more than a man's goods and chattels; this is something you will have discussed on your first visit with the minister. If it is included, the bride's father may now join his wife in the front pew, or he can stay where he is until the couple have been pronounced man and wife.

Now come the marriage vows, and again there are

alternative versions, which your minister will have discussed with you both. It is also possible in some churches to write your own vows, or to adapt the traditional words to suit. The modern service leaves out the bride's promise to "obey," which most couples now feel is outdated. The minister addresses the groom first, and then the bride, and in turn they repeat the minister's words, which are delivered in short phrases:

"I [name] take you [name] to my wedded wife/ husband, to have and to hold from this day forward, for better for worse, for richer for poorer, in sickness and in health, to love and to cherish, till death us do part, according to God's holy law, and thereto I plight my troth."

Now the minister takes the ring or rings from the best man. He offers the ring to the bridegroom, who puts it on the third finger of the bride's left hand. He holds it there while he repeats after the minister:

"With this ring I you wed, with my body I thee honor and all my worldly goods with you I share. In the name of the Father and of the Son and of the Holy Ghost."

If there are two rings, the bride now puts the groom's ring on his finger and repeats the minister's words.

The couple are pronounced man and wife, and sometimes the minister suggests that they kiss, at which point the bride lifts her veil, if she has not done so before.

After a blessing and prayers, the organ strikes up the music for the recessional – the procession down the aisle. The bride and groom lead the way, and the others fall in behind as follows:

Bride + Groom
Flower girl + Ring bearer
Maid of Honor + Best Man
Bridesmaids
Mother + Father of the Bride
Mother + Father of the Groom

## Roman Catholic

Once the bride has processed up the aisle, the service begins with a hymn and a Bible reading, followed by a sermon. The priest then asks whether there is any impediment to the marriage, and calls on the couple to give their consent to it "according to the rite of our holy mother the Church." Each responds: "I do."

Bride and groom then join right hands to make their vows, which begin "I call upon these persons here present to witness that I [name] do take thee [name] . . . ." There is no mention of "obedience" on the part of the bride. After the vows, the priest says: "You have declared your consent before the Church. May the Lord in his goodness strengthen your consent and fill you both with his blessings. What God has joined together, let no man put asunder."

Now the best man places the ring or rings on a silver salver for the priest's blessing. The groom takes the bride's ring and says: "[Name] take this ring as a sign of my love and fidelity." Putting the ring on the bride's left thumb, he says: "In the name of the Father," putting it on the index finger, "and of the Son,' on the middle finger, "and of the Holy Spirit," and finally on the third finger: "Amen."

If the bride is giving a ring to the groom, she then repeats this last section of the ceremony.

After the rings have been exchanged there are bidding prayers and a nuptial blessing; possibly also Holy Communion and thanksgiving. After a final blessing comes the dismissal, whereupon the bride and groom go with their two witnesses to the sacristy to sign the register. If there is no Mass to follow, the immediate families and other attendants also go to the sacristy; if there is to be a following Mass, the bridesmaids take their places in a reserved pew at the front.

For the Nuptial Mass, the bride and groom return to the sanctuary to kneel. If the bride is wearing a long dress and train, she may need some assistance from the maid of honor at this point; in any case, the bridegroom should support her as she kneels and rises. (It is a good idea to practice these simple actions, as they are surprisingly difficult to achieve with grace and poise.)

If Holy Communion is to be received, those taking it stand at the appropriate time and come forward, returning afterward to their pews.

When the Mass ends, the bride and groom process down the aisle from the sanctuary, with the maid of honor and best man falling in behind them, then the bridesmaids and pages. The parents of the bride and groom and other immediate family should be allowed to leave the church before the other guests make their exit.

## Quakers
The Quaker wedding is quite different from the

traditional Christian or the Roman Catholic ceremonies. Weddings between members of the Religious
Society of Friends, or Quakers, as they are called, can
take place at almost any time of day and in almost any
place, such as a private house or a meeting room, as long
as they fulfill the legal stipulations required of all
weddings. The usual choice of place is the Meeting
House normally attended by one or both parties.

The Meeting House may be decorated with cut
flowers, by the bride's mother or by a florist, but the
bride rarely wears a traditional wedding dress and
tuxedos are never seen. The bride wears her best
clothes, and the groom a gray suit with a boutonniere.
There is no procession, no music, and no minister. The
bride and groom sit at the front of the Meeting House,
facing the congregation, some of whom will be regular
attendants at the Meeting, and some wedding guests,
who may not be members of the Society of Friends and

will have little idea of the Quaker form of silent worship.
For their benefit, it is useful to include with the wedding
invitation a leaflet published by the Society of Friends
that explains the nature of the service.

The couple sit surrounded by their family and friends,
and wellwishers may get up and speak from time to time,
if they are moved to do so, or they may keep silent.
When the couple feel the moment is right, they get up
and make their pledges, holding hands.

The groom says: "Friends, I take this my friend
[name] to be my wife, promising through divine
assistance to be unto her a loving and faithful husband,

until it should please the Lord by death to separate us."

The bride then makes her vow, substituting his name and promising to be a faithful wife. The words "through divine assistance" may be replaced with "with God's help."

An alternative vow is: "Friends, I take this my friend [name] to be my wife, promising through divine assistance and so long as we both on earth shall live, to be unto her a loving and faithful husband."

Either of these two forms may be used, but no other vows are recognized, and both partners must use the same form, which will have been agreed upon beforehand with the Elders of the Meeting House.

There is no set moment for putting on a ring or rings. Some couples do it once their vows have been exchanged, others wait until the Meeting has ended and the register is signed.

After the vows, the couple sit down, and the Meeting continues as before, with some being moved to speak and others remaining silent, until two of the Elders shake hands, which is a sign that the Meeting is over. Then a marriage certificate which has been prepared beforehand, on parchment and in beautiful script, is signed by the couple and two witnesses. It is read aloud, then signed by all present and given to the couple as a memento of the occasion.

The marriage is registered by the registering officer present, and the entry is signed by the bride and groom and their two witnesses.

After this, there may be a reception in the rooms adjoining the Meeting House, and it is customary for all those present at the ceremony, even if they were not wedding guests, to be welcomed. Quakers are generally teetotal, but in some cases alcoholic drinks may be served.

## The Jewish ceremony

The Jewish wedding can take place at any time of the day – except on the Sabbath (from sunset on Friday until sunset on Saturday), and in any place, but it is usually solemnized in a synagogue.

As with other marriages, a civil licence must be obtained, but there are also several formalities that need to be arranged with the rabbi. Jewish religious law has its own rules about degrees of consanguinity (blood relationships) within which marriage may be permitted, and other religious qualifications must be met.

On the Sabbath before the wedding day, the bridegroom and his father attend the synagogue along with the bride's father and other close relatives, and the groom and one or two others are called upon to read from the Pentateuch. The bride visits the *mikveh*, a pool used for ritual purification, before the wedding.

The bride and groom usually fast on their wedding day in repentance of past sins and offer prayers for their new life together. The groom, and all other males in the synagogue, must wear some covering on their heads, as must women attending an Orthodox synagogue. The bride wears a traditional white or ivory wedding dress with long sleeves and a veil. The wedding ring is considered so important a part of the ceremony that the bride wears no other ornament, not even her engagement ring.

The wedding ceremony differs slightly according to whether it is an Orthodox or a more liberal community, but basically it proceeds as follows. The ceremony takes place in the presence of a *minyan* – a quorum of at least ten adult males. In good time before the ceremony, the groom arrives with his best man, his father, and the bride's father. They take their places in front of the congregation by the *chuppah*, the wedding canopy of silk or velvet which is held up by four poles. The chuppah is a relic of the time when the children of Israel lived in tents. It symbolizes the bridal chamber; to some it signifies the home the couple will make together; its fragility reminds the couple of their own weakness and of the need to nurture their union to guarantee its survival.

When the bride arrives at the synagogue, the groom and his best man step under the chuppah while the two fathers go to greet her. They then process up the aisle, the bride on the arm of her father, the bridesmaids behind, then the groom's parents, and the bride's mother, escorted by a male relative. Singing may accompany the procession, and Psalms 80 and 100 are often chosen for this occasion.

The bride joins the bridegroom under the canopy, standing on his right. The other escorts stand around the couple according to instructions given them beforehand by the rabbi. All face the Ark, which is on the east side of the synagogue. The rabbi welcomes and blesses the wedding party, then there is a psalm of thanksgiving and the rabbi gives a short address. Next the rabbi gives the betrothal blessing, which is recited over a cup of wine. In some synagogues, the minister now addresses the couple saying:

"You [name] and you [name] are about to be wedded according to the law of Moses and of Israel. Will you [groom's name] take this woman [bride's name] to be your wife? Will you be a true and faithful husband unto her? Will you protect and support her? Will you love and honor and cherish her?"

The groom answers: "I will," and similar questions are asked of the bride, who also replies: "I will." In other synagogues, these questions are not part of the marriage ceremony, but are asked informally beforehand.

The most important part of the ceremony now follows. The bridegroom places the ring on the index finger of the bride's right hand, declaring: "Behold thou art consecrated unto me by this ring according to the law of Moses and of Israel." The bride is not required to say anything. Her mute acceptance of the bridegroom's ring and his vow are taken to constitute her side of the bargain, and the marriage is now complete. The bride may put the wedding ring on the third finger of her left hand later.

The *ketuba*, or marriage document, is read out, first in Aramaic (at an Orthodox wedding) or in Hebrew (in the Reformed church), and then in translation. This document includes specifications that take care of the bride financially in case of divorce or bereavement. (The Jewish faith does allow remarriage of divorced Jews, so long as the divorce has been authorized by Jewish law.)

The Seven Benedictions are then sung or recited, and the bride and groom drink wine from the same glass, symbolizing the fact that they will share all things. The bridegroom then dashes the glass to the floor and grinds it under his foot. Some say this is a reminder of the destruction of the temple in Jerusalem; others that it frightens off evil spirits; friends may call out *maazel tov* (good luck) at this point. The breaking of the glass may also symbolize the fragility of marital happiness.

Before the end of the ceremony, a covenant is signed, which reads:

"On the . . . day of the week, the . . . day of the month of . . . in the year . . . corresponding to the . . . of . . ., the Holy covenant of marriage was entered into . . ., between the bridegroom . . . and his bride . . .

The said bridegroom made the following declaration to his bride: "Be thou my wife according to the law of Moses and of Israel. I faithfully promise that I will be a true husband unto thee. I will honor and cherish thee; I will work for thee; I will protect and support thee; and will provide all that is necessary for thy due sustenance, even as it beseemeth a Jewish husband to do. I also take upon myself all such further obligations for thy maintenance during thy lifetime as are prescribed by our religious statutes."

And the said bride plighted her troth unto him, in affection and with sincerity, and has thus taken upon herself the fulfillment of all the duties incumbent upon a Jewish wife.

"This covenant of marriage was duly executed and witnessed this day according to the usage of Israel."

Finally there is a blessing and a psalm of praise. The couple sign the register and retreat to a private room to spend a few moments alone together. During this time, they may share a bowl of soup to break their fast. Afterward they leave the reception, at the end of which the Seven Benedictions are repeated.

## A civil ceremony

Brevity and simplicity are the keynotes of a civil ceremony. The proceedings take only a few minutes.

The bride and groom may dress in traditional wedding outfits, but the groom is more likely to wear a suit and the bride a street-length dress. A small party of close friends and relations usually witness the ceremony.

## The Buddhist ceremony

Buddhist traditions are likely to be combined with local ones. The bride will probably wear a dress with a veil for the ceremony, and there will be a reception afterward. Guests send presents and wear dressy clothes.

Before the ceremony, chanting greets the guests, who are ushered into their places by girls wearing white. Then the bride and groom arrive and are escorted by a lay leader to a holy cabinet containing a sacred scroll. They kneel before this and perform the ceremony of Gong-yo, which consists of reciting sutras and chanting for about 15 minutes.

Then each sips three times from three bowls of increasing size, to symbolize how their lives will grow and expand together. There may be an exchange of rings, after which the lay leader will explain the meaning of a Buddhist marriage. At the end of the ceremony, the guests clap and cheer.

## The Hindu ceremony

A Hindu wedding may last all day, and there may be hundreds of guests, so the event usually takes place in a rented room. Guests wear their best clothes – the women in gold-embroidered saris, and men may also wear bright colors – but the ceremony is quite informal, and guests laugh and talk among themselves while it is going on.

In the middle of the room, the bride's family will have set up a "sacred place," covered with a canopy of brocade or some other richly decorated material and festooned with flowers. The bride, wearing a red silk sari, is the first to arrive, but she hides out of sight until the bridegroom, robed in white, has been brought with his friends and relations. As he enters, lights are waved over his head and grains of rice are thrown, symbolizing riches and fertility, then he takes his place under the canopy. The bride is brought out to join him, and close friends and relations may also cluster around.

Presents may be sent in advance or they can be brought along to the wedding and given personally to the bride or groom.

## The Muslim ceremony

Muslim men can marry Muslim, Christian, or Jewish women, but Muslim women may marry only Muslim men. The Muslim wedding takes place in a mosque and is usually, but not necessarily, conducted by an imam. As the Islam wedding is a contract and not a sacrament, a lay Muslim male may officiate at the ceremony.

The bride dresses in red, the groom in a dark suit, and the guests wear dressy clothes, sometimes also hats. The women gather on one side of the mosque, the men on the other. A sermon is followed by a reading from the Koran, and then the bride and groom give their consent to marry. They are pronounced man and wife. There is a further sermon and prayers, then all the guests are given a sweetmeat, usually dried dates or figs, before leaving.

Afterward there is a reception hosted by the bride's parents, and friends and relations of the bride bring presents. A week later, the parents of the groom host a similar party, and his friends and relations bring their gifts.

## Double weddings

Twins, siblings, or close friends sometimes choose to get married at the same ceremony and share the same reception to underline the bond that exists between them. Obviously, this cuts the cost of the reception and other attendant expenses, which in the case of the two consecutive weddings would be very great. It also halves the amount of admiration and attention given to each bride, which some may feel to be a drawback.

The brides should wear complementary outfits, either both dressing traditionally or both in dressy day clothes, so that neither upstages the other. Each couple may have their own attendants, or they may share; though each should have their own best man, to avoid confusion with the rings – then bridesmaids. If the brides are sisters, then the elder takes precedence; if they are not, then the elder groom and his bride are attended to first.

If the brides are sisters, and their father is required to give each of them away, he may escort first one, then the other up the aisle. Alternatively, the brides may choose to omit the "giving away" ritual from the ceremony and proceed up the aisle side by side, with their attendants following.

Both grooms wait at the front of the church, each with his best man. As the first bride arrives, the attendants must be careful not to get in each other's way and especially careful not to block the progress of the second bride. The numbers of attendants may be limited by the size of the church, and there will need to be at least one careful rehearsal.

The ceremony proceeds in the normal way, until the time comes when the couples are required to give their responses. The senior couple completes its vows first, and the junior follows.

The procession down the aisle is the most complex maneuver in a double wedding. Some couples prefer to allow the first bridal party to complete their exit with their attendants before the second party moves down the aisle; others prefer that the first bride and groom should be followed immediately by the second couple, with their attendants in pairs behind them, first the maid of honor and best man of the first couple, then those of the second couple, etc. The parents of each bride, and then the parents of each groom, leaves the church in the same order as the couples.

The order of procession and the escorts are a matter of individual preference; the important thing is that it should be decided with tact and thoroughly rehearsed, so that no one is offended or left not knowing which way to turn.

## Seeing off the happy couple

In past times it was customary to shower the bride and groom with petals as they left the church, and for them to walk along a path strewn with flowers. This charming idea gave way to the throwing of rice, to symbolize fertility and plenty. This does not cause a litter problem as the birds will eat it, but it can hurt if flung with great vigor. Nowadays, many people choose to throw bird-seed, or mixed seed and rice, or you could always go back to a shower of petals! Small net bags of your chosen good-luck grain can be given to guests as they leave the church or reception. You may choose to leave the church through an aisle made by well wishers. Military brides walk under an archway made of swords, but if you or the groom has a hobby such as rowing or tennis, you could have an archway of oars or rackets.

# 8 THE RECEPTION

The bridal party (all but the best man, who stays on to make sure that there are no problems, and, if it is has not already been done, hand over the minister's fees in a sealed envelope) make their exit from the church first, in order to welcome guests to the reception. The traditional manner of doing this is to form a receiving line, so that each guest is greeted by each key member of the bridal party. The chief participants line up near the entrance door as follows:

Bride's mother
Groom's father
Groom's mother
Bride's father
Groom
Bride
Maid of honor
Bridesmaids

Guests of the bride who do not know the groom's parents are introduced to them by the bride's parents as they are passed along the line; guests who do not know the bride's parents are introduced in similar fashion by the parents of the groom. There is no time to exchange family news; all that is expected are congratulations and good wishes.

If the reception is large, the receiving line inevitably takes a great deal of time, and the first guests to arrive may have to wait a considerable time for refreshment, while the last face is standing outside in line in what may be less than pleasant weather. With a double wedding, the delay can be interminable. Nowadays, the receiving line can be replaced by a welcome from the bride's mother alone, or from the newlyweds. The other members of the bridal party can circulate, which allows for longer, more natural conversations as well as for new introductions. If you do have a receiving line, arrange for drinks to be offered to the guests as soon as they have passed it.

Another alternative is to have all the bridal party circulating, and have each guest announced by a toastmaster as he or she enters. Both these methods allow the reception room to fill up quickly, for the host family to put people at their ease and make sure that everyone is offered a drink, and avoid the need for divorced parents to stand together and perform pleasantries.

Some guests may arrive with presents, so there should be a table near the entrance on which they can be put for opening later. Make sure any cards remain with the correct presents; you could give a friend some adhesive tape and ask her to see to this!

## The festivities

The guests should be offered something to drink as soon as they arrive, and appetizers to bridge the gap to the meal. As it is possible that half the people present will not know the other half, people are expected to mingle and introduce themselves. The bride and groom should try to say a few words to everybody during the festivities.

If there is a buffet, once all the guests are present, the bride's father will probably call for attention and invite everyone to help themselves. The bride and groom may lead the way, though few bridal couples eat much at their own reception. If a seated meal is planned, the best man, head waiter, or toastmaster announces that the wedding meal is served, and the party moves into the dining area, led by the bride and groom.

Some couples like to make a temporary exit at this point, so that after everyone is seated, they can be formally announced by the toastmaster: "Ladies and gentlemen, please stand to welcome the bride and groom, Dr. and Mrs. Avery Hothouse." The bride's friends and relations may get a special thrill on hearing her new name for the first time. On the other hand, if the bride is choosing to keep her own name, or the couple are hyphenating both names, this is a good opportunity for drawing attention to the fact: "Please welcome the bride and groom, Dr. Avery Hothouse and Ms. Camilla Flashpoint," or "Dr. Avery and Ms. Camilla Hothouse-Flashpoint."

The seating plan should be prominently displayed, so that every guest has an idea of where to go and no one is left wandering around peering at placecards. The best man can help by carrying a copy of the seating plan and steering guests who look lost to their places.

## Saying the blessing

A blessing is usually said if there has been a church wedding, though to many families who only attend church for christenings, weddings, and funerals, it may not come naturally.

If the minister is present, he should be asked to say the blessing, or it could be said by the bride's father or by anyone else chosen beforehand by the family. The best man (or toastmaster) will announce: "Ladies and gentlemen, Reverend Lovegrove will now say grace."

The prayer can be a simple one:

"For what we are about to receive, may the Lord make us truly thankful."

A good alternative is a personalized grace:

"We thank you, Lord, for your blessing on this food before us, and on the marriage of Avery and Camilla."

## The Speeches

Any speeches take place toward the end of the reception – during dessert and coffee at a seated meal, or about three-quarters of the way through a buffet. The guests should no longer be attacking their food with gusto, but they should still have a few choice morsels to toy with and cause to linger after the speech-making is over. At a buffet reception, speeches are often made immediately after the cake is cut.

It will be noted that the women traditionally say nothing, while the men speak for them. You may decide beforehand to do away with this chauvinistic practice, but make sure the principal parties are all in agreement: it will not do for the maid of honor to spring to her feet and begin a speech unless she has checked with the bride beforehand, and made sure that the best man's feelings are not hurt. If there are no bridesmaids, the best man need not speak at all. It really is a matter of individual taste. (For notes about speeches, see page 80.)

The speeches over, the best man may read some of the telegrams and other good wishes from absent friends, but only if they are really worth hearing and the guests aren't getting bored. These messages should of course be checked beforehand so that anything of a dubious or risque nature can be omitted; or the best man could read out a list of those who have sent telegrams. Be warned: if the speech-making goes on too long, it will be a sure dampener on the festive atmosphere.

By this time, the initial urgent exchanges of news with friends, which it would be a shame to interrupt, will have been completed, and guests will be feeling relaxed and mellow. It goes without saying that glasses should be filled for the toasts, and receptions at which alcohol is being served may bring out the champagne at this point.

The speeches at a wedding are no more than extended toasts, and no one who doesn't want to make a speech should feel forced to. Good wishes, words of thanks, and congratulations, as appropriate, will suffice, and few guests will be disappointed if these are kept to a minimum.

Traditionally there are three speeches at a wedding:

1. The bride's father, a male relation, or an old friend of the family toasts the happiness of the bride and groom;
2. The groom responds and toasts the bridesmaids;
3. The best man replies on their behalf.

As the first speech usually includes plenty of praise for the bride, some may choose to have it omitted and go straight to a vote of thanks from the groom to her parents.

## Cutting the cake

Just before or after the speeches, the cake is cut: this can be announced by the toastmaster or best man. The couple cut it in silence, her hand under his. Clapping and cheering may follow, and there is perhaps a kiss, with the photographer on hand to record it. Then the cake is whisked backstage to be cut (see the diagram on page 46), depending on the number of guests.

The cake is brought back in and distributed around the tables either by the waiters and waitresses or by the bride and groom, who this way will get another opportunity to exchange words with their guests.

**The farewell**

Some receptions are the prelude to an evening party with dancing. The bride and groom may leave quite soon after the cake has been circulated so that they can rest and change beforehand. Just as often, bride and groom are not present at the evening party, but en route to their honeymoon. In either case, they are the first people to leave the reception.

At the door, the bride tosses her bouquet to the bridesmaids: the one who catches it, the saying goes, will be the next to marry. Quite a skirmish can develop at this point unless the bride is careful in her aim, with female guests joining in the fray. A tactful bride will toss her bouquet to her maid of honor when there is no chance of her missing the catch.

Once the bride and groom have changed into their going-away clothes and are about to depart, the moment that they have been dreading is upon them: the discovery that their car has been decorated with messages in lipstick and shaving cream and tied with balloons, tin cans, and shoes.

You may treat the tin cans, the old shoes, and the dead fish in the engine as all part of the fun, but if you don't relish driving to your first destination advertising your newly married state, you can stop in the nearest service station and clean up the evidence.

The alternative is to leave in a chauffeured limosine. This is a much more relaxing way to begin your new life together. The day will have been hectic and emotional, and the contrast between being feted at your party and wrestling with rush-hour traffic could be something of a come-down. And if you need to be punctual for a train or plane, or have had a little too much champagne, the money it costs for a limo will be well spent. You might even put it on your wedding present list!

## Wedding announcements

The bride's parents may wish to place a newspaper announcement of the wedding. The wording can be simple:

Enderby: Hands – On December 18 at the Second Christian Church in Grassington, Jason Ogilvy Enderby to Haley, daughter of Mr. and Mrs. Henry Hands of West Grassington.

If the wedding has been quiet and unannounced, printed announcements should be sent to friends and relations:

Miss Haley Hands and Mr Jason Enderby announce that they were married quietly at the Second Christian Church in Grassington on December 18.

A less formal announcement might read:

Haley and Jason are delighted to tell you that they were married at Cruxmore Register Office on 18 December. They hope you will soon visit them at 32a Hulton Towers, East Grassington.

Newspapers carry stories of weddings, including information about the time, place, and attendants; descriptions of the dresses and flowers; and family histories, such as names and towns of parents and grandparents. Information about the couple's education and professions is usually included.

# 9 WEDDING DAY SPEECHES

The idea of giving a speech at a wedding can be a daunting one. You may never have spoken in public before, and this will be a large gathering with a great many strangers present. However, all is not as bad as it may seem. By the time you are required to stand and speak, the assembled company should be in good humor. You could hardly hope for a more appreciative audience.

The golden rules are:

Keep it brief

Keep it simple (no high oratory or grandiose flourishes)

Keep it decent

Make it entertaining.

The traditional number of speeches at a wedding is three. The first is given by the bride's father, or by a mature male relative or friend. The purpose of this speech is to wish the happy couple well. The bridegroom then delivers his thanks to the bride's parents, compliments his bride, and toasts the attendants. The third speech is by the best man, who replies on behalf of the attendants.

## Preparation for the best man

A good speech, however short, should have a beginning, a middle and an end, and what goes into it should be a matter for pondering on over two or three weeks before the wedding, rather than on the night before. Make notes of any ideas you have as you think of them; when the time comes to polish your speech, you can discard remarks that seem less relevant or fall short of being funny, and end up with something really worth saying.

Make your speech personal by referring to the bride and groom by name. You should not sound as though you are giving a "set" speech that could have been delivered at just any wedding. In addition to the bride and groom and other key members of the wedding, you may want to mention a relative who has come from a great distance or despite advanced age or illness – check with the bride and groom beforehand. If there are friends or relatives from other countries, you will win approval all around if you speak a few sentences in their language – don't worry if your pronunciation is not very good.

Decide how you are going to name the parents – should you call them by their first names, by their formal title, or simply refer to them as "Frank's parents"? A best man may not have met the bridesmaids before the wedding, and it is essential to get their names right, too, unless you are going to play safe and refer to them simply as "the bridesmaids."

A lot of people have difficulty when it comes to remembering the speech that they have prepared, rehearsed, and checked through just moments before they stand up to deliver it. The sea of expectant faces in front of you can make even the best rehearsed lines disappear totally from your head. Reading the speech from a piece of paper has the disadvantage that it will probably sound flat and unspontaneous. Memorizing it word for word is often not a good idea either, as it will sound like a prerecorded message, and this method does not allow for the unexpected, such as a child suddenly screaming its head off, or a fire engine siren outside.

If possible, memorize key points in your speech and fill in the actual words spontaneously. This is the liveliest way of presenting your material. If you feel you might dry up and forget what you intended to say, you could write a list of points on a small piece of paper and refer to it as necessary.

Some public speakers prefer to write the speech out in full on a series of index cards. Use large letters, underline key words, and write one paragraph only on each card. This will provide a natural pause as you put each card you have read to the back of the pile, and it will give you something to do with your hands. Cards are neat and look professional, and they don't rustle like paper.

When you are rehearsing your speech, stand in front of a mirror, holding your notes if you are going to use them, and watch out for irritating mannerisms, such as constantly touching your nose. Remember you may be on video! Use a tape recorder to check for verbal tics that need to be eradicated. Some people say "sort of," "like," "you know," or "I mean" between practically every other word, and if you are one of them, now is a good time to put this right. "Um" and "Er" are two other expressions you should try to avoid overworking!

If you do include a joke, tailor it to make it relevant by pretending, for example, that it happened to you. Don't use a wedding speech as an excuse to test your talents as a stand-up comic with a whole series of one-liners – one joke is enough. It goes without saying that crude and sexist jokes will be considered extremely unfunny and in bad taste, as will racist or religious jokes. After your joke, your audience should—with luck—laugh, so make sure you pause to allow for this and that your next words are not drowned by hilarity.

**Guidelines for preparing a speech**
* No speech should be longer than five minutes; three minutes is usually ample.
* Practice it a couple of times in front of a mirror.
* Make a tape recording of it and play it back.
* Avoid clichés such as "unaccustomed as I am to public speaking," "may all their troubles be little ones," and "embarking upon the sea of life."

**Delivery**
Someone – either the toastmaster or the best man – will announce the first speaker, and the following speakers will stand to respond to what went before, so the audience should be expectant and receptive each time. If it is not, wait for the noise to die down before you begin. Plunge in the moment that silence descends, or you and everybody else will begin to wonder why you are standing there.

If there is a microphone, make sure you are speaking at the right distance from it. If you stand too close, there will be explosive sounds as you breathe, but stand too far away and you might as well do without it. Nervous speakers sometimes sway as if they are hoping to take evasive action and escape, and this could cause your voice to come over first loud and then soft as your trajectory passes the microphone. If there is trouble with the sound system, such as a high-pitched whine, you will please everyone by abandoning the mike completely.

Speak so that the back of the room can hear you without deafening those at the front, and let your eyes skim the faces of your audience without fixing glassily on any one individual, though they should rest for a little on anyone you name in your speech.

## Guidelines for delivering speech

* Wait until there is silence before you begin. It is useless competing against chattering and laughter.

* Speak loudly enough to reach the people at the back of the room.

* Remember that speaking more loudly than usual will take more energy, so allow yourself to pause at suitable places to take a breath.

* Use words that you would normally use and speak in your own voice, or you may sound pompous or silly.

* Speak clearly, and a little more slowly than usual, taking care with your pronunciation; the people at the back won't be able to understand you if you mutter and slur your words.

* Stand comfortably. If it feels right, hold your glass in your hand if you are about to make a toast. It will give you something to do with your hands and assure your audience that you will not be speaking for too long.

* Look around at the assembled guests while you speak instead of staring at one fixed point, such as at someone's face or at the ceiling or floor. Look at the people to whom you are addressing the toast when you speak their names.

* Don't use slang – some people of a different generation might not understand it.

* Don't swear or blaspheme – it would be a shame to spoil the occasion for even one easily offended guest.

* Tell a joke by all means – everyone is supposed to be enjoying themselves – but don't on any account make it vulgar or even the slightest bit risqué. This is a happy occasion, but it marks a solemn commitment on the part of the bride and groom which should not be belittled. Any reference to the honeymoon or future children of the marriage is definitely out of bounds and could ruin the bride's day – and your future chances of friendship

with the couple and their families.

* If you want to raise a laugh at someone's expense, let it be at your own – at your own ineptitude as a public speaker, or your dreadful shyness. You will have your audience immediately on your side.

* Don't forget the purpose of your speech – which may be to make a toast! End by saying something like this: "I ask you then to rise and drink the health of [the bride and groom, or whoever it may be]."

## Using quotations in speeches

A suitable quotation can provide the speech-maker with something to hang his own thoughts on whether concurrent or contradictory. A quotation can also provide the basis for a joke and is sometimes funny in itself.

If you are using a quotation in your speech, avoid sounding pompous. If it is not the sort of thing you do in daily life, everyone will know you have looked it up anyway, so you might as well be prepared to admit it. You could say something like: 'That reminds me of something Mark Twain once said, or at least it reminds me that I looked it up last night . . . ."

Not all writers have been in favor of marriage, and some have viewed it with a distinctly cynical eye, so be sure that your choice is suitable.

Here are a few suggestions; there are many more to choose from:

* Is not marriage an open question, when it is alleged from the beginning of the world, that such as are in the institution wish to get out, and such that are out wish to get in.
*Ralph Waldo Emerson*

* Marriage is a wonderful institution, but who wants to live in an institution?
*Groucho Marx*

* Speech is great but silence is greater.
*Thomas Carlyle*

* Never go to bed mad. Stay up and fight.
*Phyllis Diller*

* Marriage is a step so grave and decisive that it attracts light-headed, variable men by its very awfulness.
*Robert Louis Stevenson*

* Strange to say what delight we married people have to see these poor fools decoyed into our condition.
*Samuel Pepys*

* Though marriage makes man and wife one flesh, it leaves 'em two fools.
*William Congreve*

**Wedding toast to the bride and groom**
This is usually proposed by the bride's father, or by a mature male friend or relative. Traditionally, he praises the bride, congratulates the groom on his luck (women are thought to deserve the best, and men to be lucky if they get it), and wishes the couple a long and happy marriage.

The speech might run along these lines:

"Ladies and gentlemen, no wonder you all look so happy. Who could not be so with two such smiling faces in the room as we see on Wayne and Suzanne? I must say that as Suzanne's doting uncle, I was prepared to be highly critical of the young man who wanted to marry her, but when I discovered that I had introduced them myself, you can imagine that all my doubts on that score disappeared.

"Wayne is a fine young man with a discerning taste – look at the wife he chose – and I'm sure he will make Suzanne a first-rate husband. As for Suzanne herself, everyone can see that she's the perfect bride – indeed she's so radiant you almost need sunglasses to look at her.

"These two young people have all the qualities they need to make each other very happy, so let us add our love and good wishes, and raise our glasses: to the bride and groom!"

## Toast to the attendants

This is the groom's speech. He is expected to refer to his own happiness – and there may be a cheer as he refers to his bride in public for the first time as his wife – and to thank her parents for making possible such a wonderful day. Finally, he toasts the attendants, and thanks them for their help and support.

The groom is not expected to be funny, unless it comes naturally to him, nor to speak for very long. His speech might go like this:

"Ladies and gentlemen, I have been married now for [looks at watch] two hours and ten minutes, and if this is what married life is like, then I can tell you it suits me very well. It is a pleasure to see so many friends and relatives enjoying themselves together under one roof, and my wife and I [pause for applause!] would like to thank you all for coming to help us celebrate. I know that Suzanne is especially happy to have her Aunt Sheila here today, and I am greatly honored that she has come all the way from Australia to wish us both well. [Pause for people to look around and smile at Aunt Sheila.]

"I would like to thank John and Maureen for laying on such a lavish spread and for welcoming me so warmly into their lovely family. A word of gratitude is due to Clint, my best man, who surprised us all by proving himself such an excellent organizer [pause for exchange of smiles with best man], and I would like to thank everyone for their generous gifts – Suzanne and I hope that you will soon be visiting us in our new home to admire them *in situ*.

"Finally, I would like to propose a toast to Glenda, Pattie, and Sarah, our three dear friends who have attended Suzanne today. Ladies and gentlemen, let us raise our glasses to them."

### The best man responds

All the best man needs to do is to thank the groom on the attendants' behalf for thanking them, and to say what a pleasure his own duties have been and add his good wishes. But in fact the best man's speech is usually the major speech at the wedding. Traditionally it provides a wonderful excuse to indulge in a little light humor at the groom's expense. (It cannot be stressed too often that the bride's feelings should be respected at all times, and that she, her family, and her impending honeymoon should not form the butt of any jokes.)

The best man's speech might go something like this:

"Ladies and gentlemen, it may seem bizarre to you that since we now have equality between the sexes I am called upon to speak for Glenda, Pattie, and Sarah, who can perfectly well speak for themselves. But it is my great pleasure to do so because I can confirm that not only have they been a great help in seeing that this happy day has gone so smoothly, but their charm and beauty have added greatly to my enjoyment of the occasion.

"The duties of a best man are indeed onerous when the groom is as much in love as Wayne, but as he so kindly said, he recognized me as a man of exceptional organizational ability. Those of you who saw us rush up the aisle just ahead of the bride in our motor cycle helmets may doubt this, but it's true.

"It's easy to forgive Wayne his absent-mindedness, knowing that it is caused by love, but there is one thing I find hard to excuse: the fact that he married such a lovely girl as Suzanne. It is lucky for a forlorn bachelor like myself that her delightful attendants are here to restore my flagging spirits.

"Ladies and gentlemen, on behalf of the attendants, may I wish Wayne and Suzanne a long life and lasting happiness together!"

# THE WEDDING DAY CHECKLIST FOR KEY PEOPLE

## THE BRIDE

### Preparation
Choose attendants
Organize wedding dress and accessories
Organize attendants' outfits
Write wedding present list
Choose trousseau
Book hair salon appointment
Buy groom's ring
Set dates for showers and parties
Buy personal gifts
Write thank-you letters

With the groom, visit the minister and discuss the following:
Vows and prayers
Music
Organist
Church flowers
Rice and birdseed bags
Photographs

With her mother, organize the following:
Guest list and stationery
Site for reception
Wedding cake
Reception catering
Personal flowers: bouquet, posies, boutonniers, corsages

Photographer / Video firm
Newspaper announcements
Wedding day transportation

## On the wedding day
Give presents to attendants
Arrange for honeymoon luggage to be taken to the
    reception venue
Get to the church on time!
Walk up the aisle on father's right arm
On reaching the bridegroom, hand bouquet, gloves, etc.
    to maid of honor
Lift veil with the help of the maid of honor
Exchange vows and rings (or receive ring)
March down the aisle
Pose for photographs
Leave church for reception
Greet guests at reception
Enjoy the reception
Cut cake with groom
Change into going-away outfit
Toss bouquet and leave for honeymoon

## THE GROOM

## Preparation
See the minister with the bride
Choose the ring with the bride
Appoint best man and ushers
Allow best man to organize bachelor party
Plan wedding suit
Plan honeymoon
Plan transportation to church and from reception
Buy personal gifts
Plan speech for reception
Pay for personal flowers

## On the wedding day
Give best man and ushers their presents
Arrange for going-away clothes and luggage to be taken
  to reception
Arrive at the church with best man 20 minutes before
  wedding
Exchange vows and rings (or give ring)
Pose for photographs
Greet guests at reception
Propose toast to attendants
Cut cake with bride
Change into going-away outfit

### THE BEST MAN

## Preparation
Check that groom has documentation for wedding and
  honeymoon
Check groom has paid for flowers, bought ring, arranged
  fees
Check that there is a private room where the couple can
  change at the reception site
Check transportation

## On the wedding day
Check bridegroom has luggage and going-away clothes
  at reception
Check going-away car is at reception site
Have ring(s) ready to hand to the minister
Have wedding documentation ready
Get groom to church 20 minutes before wedding
Pay minister's fee
Leave church for reception with maid of honor
Give speech
Read telegrams if wanted

# INDEX